A PAINFUL PAST

31-Day Devotionals for Life

A Series

Deepak Reju
Series Editor

Addictive Habits: Changing for Good, by David R. Dunham
After an Affair: Pursuing Restoration, by Michael Scott Gembola
Anger: Calming Your Heart, by Robert D. Jones
Anxiety: Knowing God's Peace, by Paul Tautges
Assurance: Resting in God's Salvation, by William P. Smith
Chronic Illness: Walking by Faith, by Esther Smith
Contentment: Seeing God's Goodness, by Megan Hill
Doubt: Trusting God's Promises, by Elyse Fitzpatrick
Engagement: Preparing for Marriage, by Mike McKinley
Fearing Others: Putting God First, by Zach Schlegel
Forgiveness: Reflecting God's Mercy, by Hayley Satrom
Grief: Walking with Jesus, by Bob Kellemen
Hope: Living Confidently in God, by John Crotts
Marriage Conflict: Talking as Teammates, by Steve Hoppe
Money: Seeking God's Wisdom, by Jim Newheiser
A Painful Past: Healing and Moving Forward, by Lauren Whitman
Parenting & Disabilities: Abiding in God's Presence,
by Stephanie O. Hubach
Patience: Waiting with Hope, by Megan Hill
Pornography: Fighting for Purity, by Deepak Reju
Singleness: Living Faithfully, by Jenilyn Swett
Toxic Relationships: Taking Refuge in Christ, by Ellen Mary Dykas

A PAINFUL PAST

HEALING AND MOVING FORWARD

LAUREN WHITMAN

P U B L I S H I N G

P.O. BOX 817 • PHILLIPSBURG • NEW JERSEY 08865-0817

Page design by Julia Myer
Typesetting by Angela Messinger

Printed in the United States of America

Library of Congress Cataloging-in-Publication Data

Names: Whitman, Lauren, author.
Title: A painful past : healing and moving forward / Lauren Whitman.
Description: Phillipsburg, New Jersey : P&R Publishing, [2020] | Series: 31-day devotionals for life | Includes bibliographical references. | Summary: "Do you live with regret? Have others sinned terribly against you? The gospel transforms your understanding of the past, your life in the present, and your hope for the future"—Provided by publisher.
Identifiers: LCCN 2020026329 | ISBN 9781629957463 (paperback) | ISBN 9781629957470 (epub) | ISBN 9781629957487 (mobi)
Subjects: LCSH: Regret—Religious aspects—Christianity—Prayers and devotions. | Healing—Religious aspects—Christianity—Prayers and devotions.
Classification: LCC BV4909 .W5 2020 | DDC 248.8/6--dc23
LC record available at https://lccn.loc.gov/2020026329

Contents

Your Secure Future

Tips for Reading This Devotional

EARLY IN OUR marriage, my wife and I lived on the top floor of a town house, in a small one-bedroom apartment. Whenever it rained, leaks in the roof would drip through the ceiling and onto our floors. I remember placing buckets in different parts of the apartment and watching the water slowly drip, one drop at a time. I put large buckets out and thought, *It'll take a while to fill them.* The water built up over time, and often I was surprised at how quickly those buckets filled up, overflowing if I didn't pay close enough attention.

Like rain filling up a bucket, this devotional will surprise you. It may not seem like much—just a few verses every day. Drip. Drip. Drip. Yet a few drops of Scripture daily can satiate your parched soul. The transformative power of God's Word will build over time and overflow into your life.

Why does a devotional like this make such a difference?

We start with Scripture. God's Word is powerful. Used by the Holy Spirit, it turns the hearts of kings, brings comfort to the lowly, and gives spiritual sight to the blind. It transforms lives and turns them upside down. We know that the Bible is God's very own words, so we read and study it to know God himself.

Our study of Scripture is practical. Theology should change how we live. It's crucial to connect the Word with your struggles. Often, as you read this devotional, you'll see the word *you* because Lauren speaks directly to you, the reader. Each reading contains at least one reflection question or practical suggestion. You'll get much more from this experience if you answer the questions and do the practical exercises. Don't skip them. Do them for the sake of your own soul.

Our study of Scripture is worshipful. As you study your Bible, you will learn that God has a lot to say about a painful past. Maybe your experience includes something on this list: feeling hurt, pain, anger, bitterness, or shame; experiencing flashbacks; replaying scenes in your mind; asking "what if?" or "why, God?" questions. Perhaps your sins and foolish decisions of the past still affect you. Or perhaps the wrong things people did to you resurface as hurt and confusion in your heart. Regardless of which description is more apt, know that God's story—the great story of Jesus coming to rescue a people for himself—applies to you. It's not just an abstract truth. It's a tender and sweet whisper of a God who says, "I know you are hurting. I know your past. I care so much I sent my one and only Son for you." What you'll find as you read the Bible is that this gentle, compassionate, loving call of our merciful God is written all over the pages of Scripture. It's probably hard for you to imagine moving from a place of hurt and deep pain to a place of healing. But through Christ, it *is* possible. My hope is that God's words, as you read them over the coming month, will provoke you to worship him.

If you find this devotional helpful (and I trust that you will!), reread it in different seasons of your life. When hurt or pain resurfaces in your life, work through the devotional again. Read Lauren's book this coming month, and then come back to it a year from now to remind yourself about what God and the gospel teach us about dealing with your painful past.

After reading and rereading Lauren's devotional, if you want more gospel-rich resources about dealing with your painful past, she has listed several at the end of the book.

That's enough for now. Let's begin.

Deepak Reju

Introduction

"*Everyone* has *something* in the past that they're not proud of."

"We all come to Christ as broken people."

"What happened to you in the past doesn't define you if you are a Christian."

Have you ever heard statements like these? My guess is that you have, and that they didn't help you. It's not that they're untrue—in fact, they are true—it's just that when you hear them, they sound like they couldn't possibly be true *for you*. Sure, everyone has something in their past. But your past, your history, feels different. Sure, other people have sinned or had bad things happen to them, but what happened in your life isn't a run-of-the-mill story. So while other people might hear those statements and be comforted, you hear them and have a different reaction. Your internal dialogue revs up:

"Yeah, but not everyone has the past I have."

"Yeah, but some of us are more broken than others."

"Yeah, but you don't know how people hurt me. It most certainly set the course for my entire existence."

These "yeah, buts" are why you picked up this devotional. Though it is true that no one comes to Christ clean, maybe you feel like a special case. Your past seems to stick to you, even though you have heard words of comfort many times before. You might be able to accept that these truths are true for others, but you're convinced that they can't possibly be true for you. You hear the words, but no comfort is in them. Nothing seems to shake your sense that you are scarred, dirty, shameful.

And so you've decided to read this book. But is it for you?

After all, a "painful past" could mean many different things. Indeed it could. I have written this book for you if

> you feel a lot of *regret* about the past—
> - choices you wish you had not made
> - choices you wish you *had* made
> - opportunities you lost
> - dreams you did not accomplish
> - failed relationships
> - missed chances
>
> you were terribly *sinned against* by others—
> - who abused you
> - who bullied you
> - who harmed you emotionally or spiritually
> - who were unfaithful to you or betrayed you
>
> your history includes pain borne from *your own sinful choices*—
> - sexual immorality
> - adultery
> - an addiction
> - substance abuse

Do you see yourself in one of these lists? Maybe you even see yourself in more than one category. I do. This issue of a painful past is true for so many of God's people for so many reasons. And thankfully, he has much to say to each of us. The curse of sin reaches far and wide, but the Lord's kindness and concern go farther still. You and your suffering are on his heart. Because you are on his heart, he stands ready to both comfort you and bring you hope.

The title of this book uses the words *healing* and *moving forward*. Think of these verbs as being in the present progressive tense. What does that mean for us? It means that the process of healing and moving forward is a work in progress. Because it is a work in progress, I have sought to write the book in such a way that it's helpful to you no matter where God has you on the healing path. It may be the first time you are seeking to understand and work through your history, or you may have done a lot of work already to heal from the past. No matter where you are, this book can help.

God has already begun his work of healing you, and he will continue to heal you over a lifetime. He uses a myriad of ways and people to help you to grow and flourish. So see this book as one tool he can use to bring about greater healing in your life. It will serve you well alongside other means of grace, such as sharing your life and story with trusted believers or working through your past with a trusted counselor over a season of months.

To prepare you, know that this book may stir up upsetting emotions, especially on days I ask you to think about details of what happened and how you have been impacted. I know both personally and from walking with others in my role as a counselor that facing the past can lead to distress or grief, even if you have reckoned with the past before. To prepare for that possibility, will you identify someone today for you to reach out to if you need to talk? If you find yourself battling hopelessness, that is definitely a time to reach out to someone. I don't want you to face heartache alone.

As you get started, will you also identify small ways to take care of yourself on days you feel sad, such as eating a favorite meal or watching a fun movie? I want you to find some relief and enjoyment if you are struggling. Know, too, that it is OK to step away from this devotional for a day or a few days to get some emotional rest. Go at a pace that makes sense for you.

Although the journey we are on may be hard, I believe it is worth it because it is based on these foundational truths:

- When we carry *a sense of regret* that our lives do not amount to all they could have, the Lord has compassion on our broken hearts. He has compassion for you.
- When we have been *mistreated by others*, the Lord cares and moves toward us. He moves toward you.

- Even when we have incurred suffering and hardship from *our own sins and choices,* God is still turned toward us. He is turned toward you.

My prayer for each of us is that these truths will increasingly become more vivid and precious to us as we venture through each day.

This devotional has four sections. Each works together with the rest to take you through a process of healing. First, we will spend several days considering afresh who our *God* is as a way to build up our faith and hope in him for our thirty-one days together. Next, we will move through considerations about your *past* to help you to wrestle through it and lessen some of the negative, harmful impacts it has had on you. After that, we will look at the *present*—and how God intends your faith to transform your experience of today. He gives you a new story and the right ways to understand yourself. Finally, we will ponder your eternal *future* and practice setting our sights on what will be. This practice is how we can experience both comfort and joy while we wait for God to make all things new.

The Lord is near, so let's entrust our pasts, our hearts, and our very lives to him and begin.

WHO IS YOUR GOD?

DAY 1

God Extends an Invitation

Trust in him at all times, O people; pour out your heart
before him; God is a refuge for us. (Ps. 62:8)

THINK ABOUT THE last time you received an invitation. Maybe it was an invitation to dinner at a friend's house, a birthday party, or a wedding. Whatever the event, it is nice to receive an invitation because it means you are wanted. You have been included. Your presence matters to the one who sent you the invitation.

In the Bible, God repeatedly finds ways to invite his people to himself. When the invitation comes from him, we can draw similar conclusions. He wants us to come to him. He longs to include us in his plans. Our presence with him matters to him.

In today's Scripture reading, you receive a particular kind of invitation. It's an invitation to pour out your heart. This is a different kind of invitation from ones we're used to. What does this invitation tell us?

First, the invitation implies that your heart is full. If you're anything like me, your heart is filled with a mix of emotions, fears, doubts, and longings. It's not all pretty. It doesn't all make sense. It's messy. It's tangled.

Second, God knows that your heart is tangled and messy, and he still extends an invitation. This tells us a lot about *him*. He's not saying to you, "Get your heart together, and then pour it out to me." He doesn't place that kind of condition on his invitation. Instead, you can come to him as you are. You don't have to come from where you wish you were or as you think you should be. Come as you are right now.

Third, the psalmist also says to trust God at *all* times. He is always trustworthy. He can be trusted with what is in your heart.

Let's put this all together as we begin this devotional. You have a God who wants to hear from you. He already knows what is in your heart—the emotions and hurt from your past that you still carry. He cares about what is there and wants to be near you as you face it. You can trust him with your heart. You can trust him with your messiness. In fact, he is so utterly trustworthy that the psalmist calls him a *refuge*, which is a safe place. He is a safe place for you. Think of the process of reading, reflecting on, and praying through this book as a process of pouring out your heart before God. Each day, God will invite you to bring yourself to him. As you respond to this invitation, trust that you are in the safe refuge of the God who loves you.

Reflect: What is it like for you to receive this invitation to pour out your heart?

Reflect: As you begin a devotional in which you will think about your past, what kinds of feelings and thoughts do you have?

Act: Begin to search for words that describe your heart in relation to your past. Will you share them with God?

DAY 2

God Listens to You

*I waited patiently for the LORD; he inclined
to me and heard my cry. (Ps. 40:1)*

YESTERDAY YOU RECEIVED an invitation to pour out your
heart before your God. Today's Scripture is a companion to that
invitation. If you are going to pour out your heart to someone—
to put words to what is going on inside you—then it's important
to trust that the person is listening to you. We all know what it
feels like to talk to someone and get the sense that they are not
really listening. They are distracted, with a faraway look in their
eyes. You ask yourself, "Should I keep talking? Does this person
care?" You wrap up what you're saying because there's no point in
sharing if the person isn't listening.

If we are going to pour out our hearts, it really matters that the
person we choose to speak to is listening. And so the psalmist's
declaration about God really matters: the Lord is inclined to you.

Here's a mental picture to help you get a sense of "inclined."
If someone is inclined to listen, that person is engaged and present. That person physically leans in toward the speaker. Their lean
indicates focus. Their eyes are on the one talking. This is God's
posture toward you as you pour out your heart before him. He
intently leans in to hear what you have to say. He is undistracted;
you have his attention. He values your thoughts and concerns.
What is on your heart matters to him, so he is not going to let
what you say fall on deaf ears. He cares too much.

He hears your cries. He hears every word. There are likely
things that you don't yet have words for. That's OK, because he
also understands your every groan (see Rom. 8:26–27). And his
hearing isn't the end of the interaction. No, God is going to take

what he hears from you and do something with it on your behalf. Often, all we can offer people is our listening ears, but we can't do much else to help, and we certainly can't change their situation. But God is going to take what he hears from you and help you. We may not know yet what form that help will take. But we can take encouragement from the psalmist, who knew what it was to wait patiently on the Lord. May we who need help wait patiently on the Lord, trusting he is inclined to us.

Over the next several days, we will continue to think about who God is by meeting him in the person of Christ. It is important to have a firm grasp of what our God is really like so that when he speaks to you about your past, it is easier to trust what he says. Jesus is the image of the invisible God (see Col. 1:15), so we will be intentional to notice how he interacts with real people.

Reflect: What is it like for you to picture God leaning in toward you as you pour out your heart to him? How does it make you feel to know that his posture is inclined toward you?

Reflect: When you think about your past, do you have a sense of what kind of help you need from the Lord?

Act: Pray that God will help you to trust him with your heart and to reveal your heart to him. Ask him to help you to be open and receptive to his help over the course of this devotional.

DAY 3

God Spends Time with Broken People

And when Jesus came to the place, he looked up and said to him, "Zacchaeus, hurry and come down, for I must stay at your house today." So he hurried and came down and received him joyfully. And when they saw it, they all grumbled, "He has gone in to be the guest of a man who is a sinner." (Luke 19:5–7)

IN MANY WAYS that are dear to us, Jesus is like us. He identified with us by becoming a human. He lived, worked, rested, and worshiped like we do. But because he was sinless, there are also ways he is *not* like us. This is important. It is easy to slip into thinking that we know what he must be like because we know what people are like. Or we may presume that the way we think and feel about ourselves is the way he thinks and feels about us. Though this is natural to us, we cannot import our understanding of people's ways into our understanding of who God is. When Jesus came to earth, it was our chance to see what God is really like.

Today's passage is our first snapshot of how Jesus relates to broken people with painful pasts. To fully appreciate what Jesus does in this interaction, know that Zacchaeus was a dishonorable, highly disliked man. A tax collector, Zacchaeus was widely—and accurately—known as a cheat and a crook. So think about this from a human perspective. If you knew someone like Zacchaeus, would you be friends with him? Go into his home and share a meal with him? I'd be concerned about my reputation. If people saw me with Zacchaeus, what would they think of me? The last place I'd want to be is in his home.

Jesus doesn't share my concerns. In front of a crowd, he initiates a conversation with Zacchaeus. He's personal and calls

Zacchaeus by name. Jesus needs a place to stay and chooses Zacchaeus's home. Zacchaeus responds immediately to Jesus's call. He welcomes Jesus to his home. He acknowledges his sinfulness, repents, and identifies a way to make up for how he has mistreated others.

Let's go back to our human way of thinking. We can easily understand the grumblers' words in verse 7. Why *is* Jesus willing to be the guest of a sinner? It would be hard to know the answer to that question if Jesus were like us, a mere man. It makes no sense for Jesus to risk his reputation by associating with Zacchaeus. Surely there is something better he could be doing—*someone* better he could spend his time with. But Jesus isn't like us. He's unafraid of being associated with sinners. Why? Because he's holy. And Zacchaeus's unholiness—and our unholiness—is no threat to Jesus. *Holy consumes unholy*[1]—but it can't go the other way. The direction is essential. We can't make Jesus unholy with our unholiness, but he can make us holy when he comes close to us and unites with us. That day, Jesus came close to Zacchaeus and united him to the holy life through the forgiveness of sins.

This story ends well. Zacchaeus joyfully responds. His friendship with Jesus makes a new man out of him.

Reflect: How do you think Zacchaeus feels about his past?

Reflect: What sticks out to you in this story about how Jesus interacts with Zacchaeus?

Act: Think about how God relates to broken people, and then write down the words that come to mind. If you were to imagine how Jesus might approach you, how would you envision that interaction?

DAY 4

God Heals Suffering People

There was a woman who had had a discharge of blood for twelve years. . . .
She had heard the reports about Jesus and came up behind him in the
crowd and touched his garment. For she said, "If I touch even his garments,
I will be made well." And immediately the flow of blood dried up, and
she felt in her body that she was healed of her disease. (Mark 5:25–29)

LET'S INHABIT THIS woman's world for a moment. She has a physical illness—an "issue of blood." She has suffered a long time, bleeding with no cure for twelve years. Imagine her daily life. The blood is always with her. She has to deal with it, clean herself, clean her clothes (in a day before washing machines). But that's not all. In her culture, her blood issues mean she is considered unclean. Thus, she must live on the outskirts of town. She has been exiled, separated from her family and home. Most tragically, her issue takes away her freedom to enter the temple to worship God. My heart aches for her.

Reflecting on this woman's hardship helps us to understand the act of desperation we witness from her. She has heard about Jesus. She has heard he is nearby. *She has faith.* She believes he has the ability to do something in her life. Crowds surround Jesus, but she presses forward and reaches out to his cloak that trails behind him. When she touches it, what happens? Power! Power goes out from Jesus, and the woman is miraculously healed.

We know, too, that the woman had been alienated from her community because of the concern that her uncleanness would make others unclean. So her touching Jesus should have made him unclean. But the opposite happens. Jesus's cleanness, so to speak, makes her clean! His holiness overcomes, blots out, obliterates all that ails her. It's like what we saw yesterday when Jesus

21

publicly associated with Zacchaeus and went into his home to eat with him. Zacchaeus's moral uncleanness was overcome, blotted out, obliterated by Jesus's moral cleanness.

When Jesus stopped, he intentionally initiated a conversation with the woman that everyone could hear. Why did he do that? By making sure everyone knew that this woman had been healed, he enabled her to be restored to her community. Restored to her home. Restored to participation in temple worship. Jesus cared about her physical suffering, and so he healed her. He also cared about her future, and so he made sure everyone knew she was healed so that she could live a different life moving forward.

Those of us with a painful past can relate to this woman's desperation. Let's borrow her faith as well. Jesus was the only one who could help her, and she trusted that he would turn toward her when she came. *Jesus, help us to trust that you are turned toward us, too.* As she reached out to him, Jesus created a new reality for her, and her life changed that day. *Jesus, we believe you want to do the same for us. Thank you for creating a new living reality within us.*

Reflect: What sticks out to you in today's story about Jesus, and thus about God?

Act: As you think about how Jesus interacts with the two people from the past two days, does it cause you to reevaluate how you might think, fear, or assume God relates to people with painful stories?

DAY 5

God Has Power over Death

[Jesus] said, "Father, I thank you that you have heard me. I knew that you always hear me, but I said this on account of the people standing around, that they may believe that you sent me." . . . "Lazarus, come out." The man who had died came out. (John 11:41–44)

YOU MIGHT HAVE noticed a pattern to the passages of the past couple days. We're looking at Jesus, but we're getting to know him as we see him *in relationship with others*. This makes sense because Jesus came from heaven to seek and to find us. God sent Jesus to mend the relationship between us and him. So of course Scripture helps us to know him by giving us stories about how he relates to us, how he knows us. And as we see how he knows us, we learn how he pursues us.

Today, we see him pursue his friend. Jesus has spent time with Lazarus and his family and is deeply grieved when Lazarus dies. Remarkably, Lazarus's story is not over. Jesus will use his power on Lazarus's behalf, just as he used his power to transform the woman's life in Day 4's passage.

Thinking about Jesus's power is humbling. This is the same person who made *everything* you can see right now. He is abundance personified! And he pours out his abundance for your sake and for mine. He shares what he has. And as we've seen with Zacchaeus and the woman with a discharge of blood, he shares his holiness. His holiness becomes theirs, just as it becomes ours. Today he shares his power for Lazarus's sake. Out of his abundant life, Jesus raises Lazarus from death.

But let's go back for a moment. Lazarus died. His life was over. Can you relate? Do you ever feel like your past has the weight of death in your life? Like there is no future for you, only darkness, only (metaphorical) death? Tomorrow, we will start part 2 of our devotional. That part might be the hardest because we are going to delve into the details of your past, and to do that probably feels like prying open a dirty tomb only to find the reeking stench of death. Because facing the past can feel this way, we've focused on Jesus these past few days. Let's put what we've seen all together so we can have the courage to open this tomb and the faith to believe there just might be life beyond this tomb.

Who is your God, and how does he relate to you?

This God invites you to speak to him.

He listens to you.

He comes close to you.

He fellowships with you.

He makes you holy.

He heals you.

He brings you new life.

Jesus is powerful—and he uses his power on your behalf.

And because all this is true, it means your *story is not over.*

Reflect: It's easy to objectively say that God is all-powerful. Is it harder to believe he would expend his power in a personal way, to benefit *you*? What makes that hard to believe?

Act: How do you describe the Jesus you've seen over these three days? Write down adjectives to describe him. Next, speak those words to him. As we move forward, ask him to be and to do what you need him to be and do on your behalf.

YOUR PAINFUL PAST

DAY 6

A Lament to the Lord

How long, O LORD? Will you forget me forever? How long will you hide
your face from me? How long must I take counsel in my soul and have
sorrow in my heart all the day? How long shall my enemy be exalted
over me? Consider and answer me, O LORD my God. (Ps. 13:1–3)

AS WE BEGIN to consider details of your painful past, I want to
offer a biblical way to think about what we are doing. The journey
we are taking is a journey of *lament*. When you first hear the word
lament, perhaps feelings like grief, anguish, and misery come to
mind. That is indeed part of what it means to lament your past.
We will recount the heartache. But a biblical lament doesn't stop
there. A lament *goes* somewhere.

Laments in Scripture "share a common structure and pattern," writes Christina Fox. "Nearly all the laments move from the
negative to positive, from sorrow to joy, and from fear to trust."[1]
A lament includes three critical movements: crying out to God,
asking for help, and responding in trust and praise.[2]

Over the next few days, we will be crying out to God about
your painful past, and that may include actual crying. It may bring
up any number of hard emotions—anger, rage, confusion, regret,
self-loathing. Today's passage gives us a sense of this first phase
of lament; it's a miserable cry from the psalmist's heart. He has
sorrow all day in his heart. From this grief, he cries, "How long, O
LORD?" In the midst of his pain, he wonders if God has forgotten
him and hidden his face from him.

I don't know if you can relate to those feelings. My point in
sharing them is not because I assume you feel that way, too. My
point is to show you that God gives you a picture here of honest
grief and of how you can share that grief with him even when it

is not tidy or theologically correct. As Christians, we know God has turned his face *toward us* in Christ. He did not forget us but made himself known to us by becoming like us. And yet today's passage creates a space for us to just cry. To be confused. To pose hard questions to God.

The next few days will likely be emotionally trying for you. So today's passage models for you what it looks like to bring yourself honestly to the Lord. You can grieve openly before him. To heal, we can't skip this first step of lament. We must cry, and we must cry out *to* God about what happened in our lives. It's the journey your soul must take. It's the journey of healing.

Reflect: Christians sometimes feel like we have to skip over the hard stuff in our lives and only reflect upon what's good and rejoice in all God has done. But God doesn't expect that from you because he knows that hard things are truly hard. He also doesn't hand you a schedule for your healing or a diagram of what that healing has to look like. He is in this with you. And he's in it with you over the long haul.

Act: The psalmist asks God questions and says, "Consider and answer me" (Ps. 13:3). When you think about the suffering you faced, and still face because of a painful past, what questions do you have for God? Personalize today's passage with your own anguish.

DAY 7

What Happened?

*[Paul] said: "I am a Jew . . . educated at the feet of Gamaliel according
to the strict manner of the law of our fathers, being zealous for God
as all of you are this day. I persecuted this Way to the death, binding
and delivering to prison both men and women, . . . and I journeyed
toward Damascus to take those also who were there and bring
them in bonds to Jerusalem to be punished." (Acts 22:2–5)*

EVERYONE HAS A story. And you and I have stories that
include a painful past. Maybe the pain was self-inflicted—you
made poor choices and suffer because of them. Maybe the pain
was inflicted upon you—you were victimized by someone who
did evil against you. The apostle Paul falls into the first category.
His painful past was due to his own sinful actions.

In Acts 22, Paul publicly shares the poor choices he made.
What were they? He breathed threats and murder against Christ's
disciples (see Acts 9:1). He entered Christians' houses and hauled
them off to prison (see Acts 8:3). He was closely connected to,
if not directly responsible for, grievous suffering in the lives of
God's people. Paul was an unjust, violent person.

On top of that, he had deceived himself into thinking that
what he was doing was actually right. If you had asked him about
what he was doing and why, he probably would have given you
many reasons why his actions were necessary and, in fact, righ-
teous. He had been well educated, after all, according to the strict
manner of Jewish law.

We know Paul did all this because he tells us. He told lots of
people, and later on in the devotional we will see why. But for now,
we will focus on the fact that Paul is honest about what happened.

Publicly declaring your sins sounds like a nightmare to me.

After all, the details of a painful past carry the stench of death. Wouldn't it be better to just bury it and run as far away as you can? I admit that it would be easier—*if* it were possible. But we can't run away from our pasts. God designed us to be impacted and shaped by our experiences. He gave us our memory, which functions amazingly well. So as nice as it might sound to just forget about what happened, it's not possible.

Over the course of this devotional, we will increasingly understand how our faith in Christ leads us to make sense of our past, present, and future story. But for today, we will call to mind the details of our past. We can't bury it. We can't run away from it. Like Paul, we have to be honest about it. I am going to ask you to be honest about it. I am going to ask you to do this in faith, trusting that together we're going somewhere good.

Reflect: You are in good company. Your brother in Christ, Paul, has gone before you in reckoning honestly with his past. He did it for good reason. You will do it for good reason too.

Act: What happened in your painful past? Over the next several days, write out the details. If there are multiple events, consider making a time line. Begin to recount what you did, what others did to you, or what happened to you that makes the past so upsetting.

DAY 8

How Did You Respond?

*Then they seized [Jesus] and led him away, bringing him into
the high priest's house, and Peter was following at a distance. . . .
Then a servant girl, seeing [Peter] as he sat in the light and looking
closely at him, said, "This man also was with him." But he denied
it, saying, "Woman, I do not know [Jesus]." (Luke 22:54–57)*

PETER'S FRIEND, PETER'S mentor, Peter's God has been
unjustly arrested and hauled away. Jesus is suffering—and Peter
watches as the devastating events unfold. Not only is it heart-
wrenching and horrific to have this happen to your friend, but it
must also be terrifying. What will happen to Peter, a friend and
follower of Jesus?

What is happening to Jesus is not Peter's fault. But as these
events take place, Peter responds in a way he will come to deeply
regret. He jumps into survival mode. His own welfare matters
more to him than the allegiance to Jesus that he had once boldly
proclaimed (see Matt. 26:33; John 13:36–37). Rather than being
a man of his word, he acts with cowardice. He lies. He denies that
he knows Jesus, not once but three times (see Luke 22:57–60).
He betrays his friend.

After Jesus dies and rises, he reunites with Peter and pursues
a deeply restorative conversation with him. Peter's forgiveness is
certain. Still, as they talk, Jesus asks Peter if he loves him. We can
understand the question. While we can appreciate the difficult
situation Peter was in on the day of Jesus's betrayal, his responses
were poor. And we, like Peter, are always accountable for our
choices. Even when something is happening around us or to us,
the choice of how to respond is ours. We choose. We aren't just
onlookers. We think, we act, we feel.

Here are two examples of how it's possible to respond to an event:

A wife has an adulterous affair. In the wake of her sinful choice, she truly repents. She confesses and seeks her husband's forgiveness. She agrees to accountability moving forward with two women at church. She enters counseling to explore the roots of her betrayal and build herself up to guard against future temptations. In short, she *responds well* after her harmful choices.

A young man, Ian, has his heart broken by his high-school sweetheart. He misses her companionship and begins serial dating. To protect himself from getting hurt again, he doesn't let anyone get to know him and moves on to the next woman before this can happen. This leaves the women he dates feeling confused and used. In short, he *responds poorly* after suffering the loss of a significant relationship.

These examples are straightforward to get you thinking, but keep in mind that our responses to events are usually mixed. We respond well, *and* we respond poorly. It's not usually one or the other. And your initial responses may differ from how you respond later. Today, be honest about how you responded to what happened in your past, just as you were honest yesterday about what happened.

Act: How have you responded to what happened? Continue to write about what happened and, as you do, also include your various responses.

Act: How are you doing with recalling your past? If you're hurting, revisit the introduction for encouragement to take care of yourself. Because God cares about you, you must take care of yourself.

DAY 9

What Are You Carrying?

When my soul was embittered, when I was pricked
in heart, I was brutish and ignorant. (Ps. 73:21–22)

IN TODAY'S PASSAGE, the psalmist brings us into his inner world. We don't know his exact circumstances, but he shares enough throughout the psalm for us to know that he had been in a bad place. His heart was so darkened that his feet "almost stumbled" (Ps. 73:2). His steps "nearly slipped" (v. 2). He was a spiritual danger to himself as he agonized over how God could let the wicked prosper. His agony was prolonged—"all the day long I have been stricken" (v. 14). The psalm is a confession of his struggles.

We can understand this confessional. When something happens to us, we respond, and then we keep on living our lives. The problem is that whatever happened doesn't go away. We have been impacted.

Remember Ian from yesterday? After his breakup, he no longer believed that loving someone was worth the risk. He didn't want to be hurt again, so he carried a guarded and self-protective attitude into his relationships. To avoid getting hurt, he hurt the women he dated by keeping them at arm's length. Similarly, after seeing the wicked prosper, the psalmist began to carry bitterness with him. And we, too, are impacted by what happened in the past.

Not only that, but we can also come to believe false messages about ourselves, others, or God because of the painful events. Ian picked up the message that he is unlovable. He feels ashamed that his girlfriend rejected him, and the message of that rejection is that there is something wrong with him. This is yet another reason he won't let other women get close to him: if they get close, maybe they, too, will see that there is something wrong with him.

But what can happen if Ian becomes aware of his cynicism and self-protectiveness and of the false messages he believes? He can fight against them. He can seek and find godly alternatives—entrusting himself to God's protection of him and repenting from protecting himself. As he entrusts himself, his future, and his relationships to God, he is free to honor women by how he interacts with them.

What are you carrying in your heart, in your beliefs, in your characteristic ways of doing life and relationships that is a result of your painful past? What messages have you received based on what happened? Now is a time to grow aware of what you are carrying. If you are not aware, then your reactions become a way of life for you. But if you are aware, then you can see what you are carrying for what it is, and you have the opportunity to do something different. You can unload what you're carrying and move forward in a new manner.

> **Reflect:** Pray and ask the Spirit to help you identify what you are carrying in your heart. Expect it to be complicated. It's likely not all your feelings will make logical sense. For example, when it comes to God, you may feel a mix of gratitude and confusion—gratitude that he got you through your past but confusion as to why he allowed it.
>
> **Reflect:** As I think about the psalmist and Ian, I feel compassion. Did you know God has compassion on you as he sees what you carry from your past? He understands, and his desire is to take away your burdens so your load is light.
>
> **Act:** Continue to write about what happened and how you responded. Now also include the different feelings, questions, and unresolved issues that you carry with you.

DAY 10

Where Was God?

Where shall I go from your Spirit? Or where shall I flee from your presence? If I ascend to heaven, you are there! If I make my bed in Sheol, you are there! If I take the wings of the morning and dwell in the uttermost parts of the sea, even there your hand shall lead me, and your right hand shall hold me. (Ps. 139:7–10)

I KNOW THAT what I asked you to look at and think about over the past three days wasn't easy. Today will also be hard. The question that we will consider may have already arisen in your mind: *Where was God?*

Or we might ask, "Why did God allow me to do what I did? Why didn't he stop me?"

Or perhaps we wonder, "Why didn't God stop what happened to me? How could he stand by and just watch?"

Avoiding questions like these seems easier to us. We think that if we remove God from what happened, we can shield ourselves from further pain. But God is unescapable. This is what the psalmist from today's passage reflects on. Wherever we are, God is there. His presence is a permanent reality. He knows all, sees all, and is sovereign over all. And he didn't stop your past from unfolding the way it did.

Why did God allow certain events to take place in your past? The question is understandable, and unfortunately I can't answer it. There are mysteries that God doesn't reveal to us (see Deut. 29:29). We don't have definitive answers to the "Why did God…" questions, but we can still bring these questions to God.

Still, there are things we *can* know for certain. Today's passage offers two reassurances for your heart that you can depend on.

First, God's hand will lead you. No matter where you are

today in your life, whether you are struggling with sin, suffering, grief, or confusion, he extends himself to you and is saying, "Let's go together from here." He leads you to places that are good. This is another invitation from him. It's as if he's saying, "Yes, I was there. I saw what happened. And you can trust me even if it feels like you can't. Will you come with me now? Can I lead you to hopeful places today?"

Second, God's right hand will hold you. You can't escape him, and he doesn't want to escape you. He wants your heart. He envelops your life with his own. He holds you, and he keeps you. It's as if he's saying, "Yes, I was there, and I know what happened. But your life is in my hands, and I will not let go of you. Will you rest because I am holding you?"

Yes, God allowed painful things to happen. And also, he is deeply tender toward you. Both statements are true. Make room for both in your heart. And make room for more comforts from the Lord. We're moving forward, and we're going somewhere good.

Act: Read the first six verses of Psalm 139, which precede today's passage. Notice God's intimate knowledge of you and the delight the psalmist takes in that knowledge.

Reflect: How can God's knowledge of everything—including his "wonderful" knowing of you—become a comfort as you think about what happened in your past?

Act: Continue to write about what happened, your responses, and what you're carrying.

DAY 11

Is There Anything You Can Do?

*Search me, O God, and know my heart! Try me and know
my thoughts! And see if there be any grievous way in me,
and lead me in the way everlasting! (Ps. 139:23–24)*

I HAD A loyal and faithful best friend growing up. She was always good to me, but I was not nearly as loyal to her. This is hard to face, especially because when I ask the question "Where was God during the years of my childhood before I became a Christian?" one of the answers is that he was caring for me through the love this friend showed me. Through the many ways she imaged our lovely Creator and showed me grace and mercy, God was with me. Years later, I wrote an apology letter to my friend. Would she forgive me for how I had failed her? She did.

When I think about the kind of friend I was, it pains me. I can't go back for a redo, and I can't erase my sins against her. But King David showed me one thing I *could* do. As he examined his life, assessing his heart before the all-knowing God, he offered today's verse as a prayer to the Lord. Just like David, I asked the Lord to know my heart accurately. Then, confident of Christ's forgiveness, I was free to be honest and say, "I see the ways I was a selfish friend." I admitted that to God and sought his forgiveness. And in my case, I had a chance to speak to my friend and seek her forgiveness as well.

It was within my power to right that wrong. Does anything come to your mind as you think about your past? Is there anything you can do now?

- Have you confessed sins from the past to God? Have you received and believed the promise of his forgiveness (see 1 John 1:9)?

- Is there anyone from your past to whom you need to confess sin (see James 5:16)?
- Is there anyone you need to make aware of how he or she sinned against you (see Matt. 18:15)? Before doing this, bring a trusted friend into the decision and seek wisdom for how to go about it. Not all situations will benefit from or require this conversation.
- Are there ways you can make restitution for damage done? Think of how Zacchaeus repaid those he had cheated.

Let's end with the last thought in today's passage: God leads us in "the way everlasting." Considering how to respond to your past is actually an aspect of what it means to be in this way everlasting. How so? Though you can't change what happened, you do have power to move forward in a manner that mitigates the negative impacts of the past. Knowing that, consider again what you're carrying from your past. It is critical to surrender negative or unhealthy behaviors and beliefs to the Lord and take up new behaviors and beliefs, ones that are congruent with the everlasting way God has you in. If you were to put down what you carry, what might the Lord have you take up?

Reflect: The apostle Paul says, "If possible, so far as it depends on you, live peaceably with all" (Rom. 12:18). This is one reason I posed some considerations above, but sometimes there is nothing left in our power we can do to be at peace with others. Maybe you've done all you can, and there is still fallout. What does it look like, then, to entrust the fallout and the broken relationships to your Father, who longs to carry such burdens?

Act: Continue to write about what happened, your responses, and what you're carrying. Now also begin to prayerfully consider and write about what you can carry instead.

DAY 12

How to Think Biblically about Your Past

As a father shows compassion to his children, so the LORD
shows compassion to those who fear him. For he knows our
frame; he remembers that we are dust. (Ps. 103:13–14)

I AM DUST. You are dust. It's not the most flattering description, is it? Dust is a nuisance, and its presence is utterly unwanted. When you touch it, you get dirty and need to clean it off. Is God trying to make us feel bad about ourselves here? Thankfully, no. Rather, these verses offer us a way to think accurately about ourselves and about who God is. God remembers we are dust, so we must remember it too—because it actually leads to good news.

On Day 5, we spoke of how our pasts bring the stench of death into our lives. Today's verses remind us of that because dust in the Bible is a symbol of our mortality. We will return to the dust one day when we die (see Gen. 3:19). In the meantime, even while we live, dust captures truth about us—especially those of us who wrestle with a painful past.

So yes, you are dust. And yes, your past has that stench of death. Your past is a confirmation of your weakness; you can't construct something strong and formidable out of your past on its own. But what is essential in today's verses is God's compassion for you. When he looks at you, and when he considers your past, his response is that of a loving father.

You might look at yourself and your past and only see "dustiness"—dirtiness, weakness, failure, and death. But that is not God's view of you.

A faithful rendering of today's passage could sound like this: "Yes, there is dust—there is frailty and death—in my past, *in my choices and in how I lived.*" Or perhaps this resonates more: "Yes, there is dust—there is death—in my past, *in how I was treated and in what happened to me.*" And here comes the good news: "But my heavenly Father has compassion on me. He knows my frame, he knows my whole story, and his posture toward me—even as he knows me completely—is merciful and kind."

This is one way to think biblically about your past. It puts the emphasis on the right person. It doesn't emphasize what you did or what happened to you. The emphasis is on your Father, who has compassion on you. The emphasis is on your Father, who takes weak, dying dust and breathes new life into it.

Reflect: We are putting a biblical lens on your story. One essential aspect of healing and moving forward is to put the emphasis on the right person. We want to know what God thinks about us. So think about your past and its details, but think about them through the lens of God's compassion for you. Imagine him considering your past and being moved with compassion for you.

Act: Read the story of the prodigal son in Luke 15. This powerful story showcases the Father's compassion for his children, no matter what happened in the past. Pay special attention to the father's joyful embrace when his son comes to him. Do you know that God's arms are open to you?

Act: Continue to write about what happened, your responses, what you're carrying, and what God would have you carry instead.

DAY 13

What God Does with Your Past

Bless the LORD, O my soul, and forget not all his benefits, who forgives all your iniquity, who heals all your diseases, who redeems your life from the pit, who crowns you with steadfast love and mercy, who satisfies you with good so that your youth is renewed like the eagle's. (Ps. 103:2–5)

A LIFE THAT is in the pit. Doesn't that resonate for those of us with painful pasts? We experience consequences, repercussions, effects, and impacts from the past, and trying to escape them feels just like trying to climb out of a pit with no ladder.

A pit is dark. It's dirty. The air doesn't circulate well at the bottom of the pit, and there's that stench of death again. What lives at the bottom of a pit? Only disgusting creatures. What can prosper at the bottom of a pit? Nothing! You cannot prosper if your life is in the pit.

What do you do? If a painful past has put your life in the pit, you may wonder, "How am I going to crawl out of this pit?" That's a natural question to ask, but it's not going to get you anywhere. Here is the right question: "Does God care that I am in this pit—and can *he* do anything about it?" This question is vital because of the reality of your human frailty. You simply can't get yourself out of that pit.

So if we look up to God from the pit, what do we find that God can do? Look at the action verbs in today's passage. This is God's activity on your behalf:

He *forgives* all your iniquities.

He *heals* all your diseases.

He *redeems* your life.

He *crowns* you with love and mercy.

He *satisfies* you with good.

And what is the effect of all his actions on your behalf? "Your youth is renewed like the eagle's." Your past, your life, is being renewed. Think of an eagle soaring high. What would a pit look like from an eagle's vantage point? The eagle could see it, but that's about all. The pit isn't a threat to the eagle. He's flying above it. He's not in it.

This is what God does with your past. He takes you out of the pit and brings you to new places where your past no longer threatens to dominate your life. Because of his activity in your life—his forgiving, healing, redeeming, crowning, satisfying activity—you are renewed. You are new. This is your new reality.

And this is where we are going next. We are going to move away from your past and into the new reality of your present— of who you are today because of the reality of God in your life. Because of the reality that there is Someone strong enough, able enough, and loving enough to rescue you from the pit.

Reflect: Reread that list of God's activity in your life when your past has put you in the pit. Take each verb in slowly. Read it out loud and personalize it—say, "He forgives all *my* iniquities," and so on.

Act: Worship through one of your favorite songs. Worshiping is a way to focus on the One who rescues you out of the pit. To get out of the pit is to take your eyes off yourself and to consider Another. He is the God who redeems your life.

YOUR TRANSFORMED
PRESENT

DAY 14

Christ Has All Authority

Now the eleven disciples went to Galilee, to the mountain to which
Jesus had directed them. And when they saw him they worshiped him,
but some doubted. And Jesus came and said to them, "All authority
in heaven and on earth has been given to me.... And behold, I am
with you always, to the end of the age." (Matt. 28:16–18, 20)

WE ARE MOVING into a new section of our devotional—the
present. As we've finished section 2—the past—my hope is that
you are walking away from it with this understanding: your past
was significant not only because of how painful it was but also
because of how it impacted you. God cares about both what happened and how you were affected, and so you have considered
what you carry from the past and what better, healthier alternatives could be. To that we will now add this truth: your story is
not over, even with the realities of your past in view. Left on your
own, you might be tempted to tell a false story about yourself,
such as "My past ruined my life" or "My past determines my
future." But God is the one who tells the true narrative of your
life. It's the story that he then wants you to tell yourself about who
you are. Your new story is his gift to you. This moves us into the
present.

In today's passage, the resurrected Christ commissions his
disciples in preparation for his departure; he will ascend soon to
his Father. Jesus calls them to a difficult future because they will
face opposition as his disciples. In light of this, notice the reassurance he gives them: "All authority in heaven and on earth has been
given to me." The disciples will go out and take risks, encounter
resistance, endure rejection, and even face death. So what good is
it that Christ has all authority? It's the encouragement that even

though there will be hardship, Jesus's disciples are connected to the One who sets the trajectory for not only them but the whole world. Christ came to earth, died, and was raised so that we could be saved and reconciled to the Father. This is the drama in which we are all living.

That brings us back to your story. Will you believe that Christ has all authority to tell your story? Perhaps it's easy to believe an abstract notion that "God is in charge." For example, it's not hard to admit that we can't control the weather or that we didn't choose where or when we were born. We're not in charge in that sense; God is. But let's get more personal. Will you believe that Christ has—and should have—all authority in *your* life because of who he is and what he has done for you?

Today's passage says that some worshiped and some doubted when they saw Christ. As we move into the present tense of your life, I want to ask you to be a worshiper of the God who has all authority. What does that mean for you? It means you are going to choose to put your stock in what this Christ says about who you are. Self-condemnation, shameful feelings, and the sense that you are a failure claim authority over who you are when you wrestle with a painful past. They dictate how you perceive yourself. But the resurrected Christ—the one with authority over all heaven and earth—is the *only* one who truly has the power to tell you who you are. And he is trustworthy.

Act: We all have moments, periods, even seasons, of doubting. The goal is to develop a habit of turning to the Lord when you doubt. Remember that a faithful lament includes crying out to God and responding in trust. When you turn to him and say, "I choose to worship you," it shows you trust what he says because he has the authority in your life. Will you practice this in the coming days when doubts cloud your present?

DAY 15

You Have a New Story

In the sixth month the angel Gabriel was sent from God to a
city of Galilee named Nazareth, to a virgin betrothed to a man
whose name was Joseph, of the house of David. And the virgin's
name was Mary. And he came to her and said, "Greetings, O
favored one, the Lord is with you!" (Luke 1:26–28)

ALTHOUGH YOU MIGHT see yourself and your story as defined by your past, that is not the way God sees you. (And remember, he is the one with the authority!) Your new story starts with Jesus's story. You are living in his story *now*. How is this so? The foundational spiritual reality of the Christian life is that *Christ brings us into himself.* He shares himself with you. He shares *all* of himself with you, including his story. His past is your past. His present is your present. And his future, too, will be yours.

Your new, present-tense story is that you belong and are connected to Christ, and your connection to him defines you now. To get a sense of your new story, take a look at the beginning of Jesus's earthly life. From what we read, we begin to understand how extraordinary his life is going to be. First, an angel delivers the birth announcement. And second, Jesus will be born of a virgin. Both details are incredible! This birth, the beginning of Christ's tale, already includes miracles, indicating that his coming is a really big deal. And we're just getting started!

But why is Jesus coming? He's coming to recreate you. He's coming so that I can write these words to you today: you have a new story.

Today's passage is good news. Someone new has come onto the scene. This new event—the coming of Christ—overlays your old story. Christ's coming to earth introduced his life into the life of the whole world and all the people in it. And when his life becomes your own, your story can no longer be told or understood in the same way.

What must you understand about your story in light of Christ's life bursting into the world? Understand that you don't have to live hopelessly because of what happened in your past. Today, you can pivot. Living with a painful past can feel like you are always oriented toward what happened. It's like your life is endlessly stuck back there. But because of the reality of Christ's coming, you can orient yourself to today and even tomorrow. His story changes everything for you—and in the days ahead, we will continue to press into the many ways this can be true in your life.

Reflect: When the angel Gabriel came to Mary, he delivered good news. Today's good news for you is that Christ offers you a new story, one that is not defined by your past. What would it look like for you to receive this good news? Is anything stopping you from believing it?

Act: Starting on Day 9, you began to consider what you are carrying. What feelings, wounds, and messages do you still carry today because of what happened in the past? What triggers them for you in the present? With these in mind, write out the story you tend to tell yourself about who you are today because of what happened in the past.

DAY 16

You Are in Christ

If anyone is in Christ, he is a new creation. The old has passed away; behold, the new has come. (2 Cor. 5:17)

As we said yesterday, the foundational spiritual reality for believers is that Christ brings us into himself. Today's verse uses that language: "If anyone is *in Christ* . . ." We are in Christ when we have looked to him in faith and trusted him to forgive our sins because of his death on the cross. And when you are in Christ, you are a new creation.

I became a Christian the month I turned twenty years old. I was completely unfamiliar with the Bible at the time, and I remember the first time I read today's verse: I was driving behind a car that had it on a bumper sticker! This was nearly twenty years ago now, but I still remember the moment vividly because the verse *thrilled* me. The idea of being new was such good news to me.

When you've lived through a painful event or lived with a painful past, this verse can bring hope in a way nothing else can. Why? Because it points to a do-over of sorts. The old is passing away. The new has come. This is a second chance. And there's nothing you have to do for it to be true. Notice how the verse states the new reality as fact: if you are in Christ, you are a new person. It's that simple. It's that profound.

Today's passage reminds me of one of my favorite Christmas hymns, "O Holy Night."[1] One verse sings,

> Long lay the world in sin and error pining,
> Till he appeared and the soul felt its worth.
> A thrill of hope—the weary world rejoices,
> For yonder breaks a new and glorious morn.

This verse describes another way to capture how Christ brings a person with a painful past into his story. Let me unpack it.

For you, your life long lay pining in sin and error. To *pine* means you are suffering with longing. Because of sin and error—either your own or the sins and errors of others that have impacted you—you are suffering. You are "weary" from the suffering. But then Christ appears! He who had been heralded by Gabriel, born of the virgin Mary. And because his appearance was to rescue you from your sin and suffering, your soul now knows its worth. You matter to him. Your life is so significant to God that he sent his only Son to come and provide a way for you to have a new life with him.

"For yonder breaks . . ." *Yonder* means "over there." This captures well what it feels like to live with a painful past because the new can feel like it's "over there" and out of reach for you. But yonder breaks . . . ! And what comes? A new and glorious morning.

This is your new story. When Christ appeared, glory dawned in your life. Your past is passing away. Behold, you are in Christ, and his story is now your own.

Reflect: Modern Western society teaches us to think of ourselves in individualistic terms. You might need to get used to thinking of yourself in terms of someone else's story. Doing so is one way the gospel is good news: it's not just you and your story that determine what your life was, is, and can be.

Act: Listen to "O Holy Night." As the song sings, "fall on your knees" and worship him who appeared in our weary world for your sake. He appeared to you so your soul could know its worth.

DAY 17

You Have a New Identity

You have died, and your life is hidden
with Christ in God. (Col. 3:3)

TODAY'S VERSE OFFERS us an interesting spiritual reality to ponder. Your life—the life you are living right now, today—is hidden in Christ. This presents a remarkable answer to the question "Where are you right now?" Spiritually, an accurate response is "I am in Christ right now!" Indeed. You are in Christ. He is where you can be found. He found you when you were lost, drifting, and far off, and he brought you into himself (see Eph. 2:1–5). He found you, and now he is where you are found.

Let's go back to the beginning of the verse: "You have died." This goes hand in hand with yesterday's "the old has passed away." The old has passed away because you have died. You died when you were crucified with Christ.

Now let's bring in another verse to help build on these ideas: "I have been crucified with Christ. It is no longer I who live, but Christ who lives in me. And the life I now live in the flesh I live by faith in the Son of God, who loved me and gave himself for me" (Gal. 2:20). You died with Christ. You no longer live, but Christ lives in you. How is that possible? By faith. You access your new life by faith.

For someone who struggles with a painful past, one area in which to live by faith is that of identity. Does your painful past define you? Does it determine what life is like today and tomorrow? In your own understanding and experiences, the answers might come quickly and confidently: "Yes, my past defines me! Yes, my past determines my life!" I know it can certainly seem that way, can't it?

This is exactly where faith must come in. Faith in the Son of God means choosing to rest in Christ's understanding of who you are. It means choosing to find relief in how Christ's story transforms yours. He loves you, and he proved it when he gave himself for you. Then he brought you into himself. This is your present-day reality. This is what Christ has accomplished in your life. And because you are found in Christ, the Father sees you in his Son, with whom he is fully pleased. You are in his Son, who is exalted and is sitting at his right hand at this very moment. Like Christ, you too are spiritually in God's very presence. The life you now live, you live by faith that you are with your Father, welcomed by your Father, and secure with him.

Reflect: Read that last sentence again. Again, this might not yet resonate with your experience. But will you accept its truthfulness *by faith*? Will you consider saying and committing to this: "Lord, I believe your Word over my own understanding of how you see me and how I see myself. And today I believe that I am in you and you are in me—and that this reality is the truest, deepest truth about myself."

Act: Listen and worship to the hymn "It Is Well with My Soul." Notice the present-tense verb in the hymn's title: it *is* well with your soul. Because Christ brought you into himself and your life is hidden in his, all is well with your soul *today*. It doesn't mean all is well in every aspect of your life. But it does mean you know where you stand with God.

DAY 18

You Are in God's Family

But to all who did receive him, who believed in his name,
he gave the right to become children of God, who were
born, not of blood nor of the will of the flesh nor of the
will of man, but of God. (John 1:12–13)

WE ARE GROWING our understanding of who we are in the present tense. Today's verse gives another way to describe you: you are *a child of God*.

How did you become God's child? Here's good news: you are a child when you receive and believe in his name. You don't become a child because you somehow prove you are worthy to be one. You don't become a child because your past is dignified and respectable. You don't become a child because God sees how desirable you are and thinks you'd be a stellar addition to his family. No, you became God's child because he saw you, he had compassion on your helpless estate, and he adopted you, bringing you into his family. And because he did, you received him. You believe him. And because you do, you have the "right" to be his child. God's actions on your behalf made a way for you to become "born of God," a member of his family.

Beloved theologian J. I. Packer describes how crucial it is to understand that God is our Father and we are his children. He goes so far as to say that "if this is not the thought that prompts and controls [our] worship and prayers and whole outlook on life, it means that [we] do not understand Christianity very well at all." Packer encourages us to use adoption as the lens through which to see the New Testament: "Everything that Christ taught, everything that makes the New Testament new . . . is summed up in the knowledge of the Fatherhood of God. 'Father' is the

Christian name for God. Our understanding of Christianity cannot be better than our grasp of adoption."[1]

How do you claim your privileged position as a child of God? You believe that it is true of you. Your understanding of who you are, of how God sees you, of why God sent Christ for you, cannot be better than your grasp of how deeply you believe and rest in your understanding that you are his child.

Do you claim this right because of what God has done for you?

Reflect: On the previous page, I borrowed the phrase "helpless estate" from the hymn we sang yesterday, "It Is Well with My Soul." Consider the whole stanza:

> Though Satan should buffet, though trials should come,
> Let this blest assurance control,
> That Christ has regarded my helpless estate,
> And hath shed his own blood for my soul.[2]

When a loving father sees his child in a "helpless estate," he springs into action. Your God, your Father, was *so* moved by you and your helplessness that he gave his own Son to make you his child. How can this reality of the Father's love for you control your outlook on your life? How can it control how you think about your past, live in the present, and look forward to your future?

Act: Pray to your Father. When you pray, call him "my Father." He is God, yes. And he also is your Father. Talk to him about how this controlling reality of his relationship to you strikes you.

DAY 19

You May Boast in the Lord

*Not many of you were wise . . . , not many were powerful, not many were
of noble birth. But God chose what is foolish in the world to shame the
wise; God chose what is weak . . . to shame the strong; God chose what is
low and despised . . . so that no human being might boast in the presence of
God. And because of him you are in Christ Jesus, who became to us wisdom
from God, righteousness and sanctification and redemption, so that, as it
is written, "Let the one who boasts, boast in the Lord." (1 Cor. 1:26–31)*

GOD CHOOSES WHAT is foolish, weak, low, and despised.

Foolish, weak, low, and *despised.* Even though these words
are unsavory descriptors, today's passage reveals a truth that we
never would've guessed: God is actually drawn to foolish, weak,
low, and despised people. After all, if you are foolish, weak, low,
and despised, then you can't boast. When we consider all God
has done for us in Christ, it is easy to understand why boasting in
ourselves is inappropriate.

I'd venture to say that you aren't boastful about what you have
done or what has happened to you in the past. The instinct is to
hide it. And yet God sees you, he sees your past, and he is drawn
to you. He doesn't despise you because you have a past that you
despise. He chooses instead to unite you with his Son, Jesus. This
is his choice. And because he made the move toward you already,
you can respond and make a move toward him. Turn toward him,
and turn away from the past.

When you turn, what do you see in Jesus? He is wisdom from
God. He is the one who became for you righteousness, sanctification, and redemption. Read that again. Jesus became wisdom *for
you.* He is *your* righteousness, sanctification, and redemption. You
are right before God; all is well between you. Christ is sanctifying

you; you are purified and freed from the terror of sin's reign in your life. Christ is redeeming you; he atoned for your guilt and purchased your soul. These truths are true for you, and they are what you can boast about!

Paul borrowed this verse from the Old Testament. In the original passage, the writer records additional words from God: "Let him who boasts boast in this, that he understands and knows me, that I am the LORD who practices steadfast love, justice, and righteousness in the earth. For in these things I delight, declares the LORD" (Jer. 9:24). I love how God wants us to be confident about who he is. We can boast that we really know and understand the Lord of heaven and earth. He is the God who practices steadfast love, justice, and righteousness—and delights in doing so! You can be certain about that. You can boast about what he is like and about who he is to you. He is the one who chose to bring you to himself and transform your life. With delight, he takes what was foolish, weak, low, and despised and makes you wise, strong in him, exalted with his Son, and cherished.

And therein is a calling on your life in the present—to boast in what Christ has done for you.

Reflect: Jesus, our sanctification and redemption, creates striking transformations: Weaknesses becomes strengths. Wretches become treasures. Wounds become glory. God is a master of transformations.

Act: Listen and worship to the hymn "How Deep the Father's Love for Us," and notice the transformations. Delight and be at peace in how God is transforming you.

DAY 20

You Have a Helper

*"The Helper, the Holy Spirit, whom the Father will send
in my name, . . . will teach you all things and bring to your
remembrance all that I have said to you." (John 14:26)*

AS WE CLOSE this section, let's put together everything we've
heard God say about who you are in the present. Christ, who possesses all authority in heaven and earth, has said and done many
things in your life. Because of him, you have a new story. Another
life and another story have become true for you. You are in Christ.
This means you are a treasured member of his family. Because of
these stunning realities, you have every reason to boast about
who Christ is and what he has done for you—because only he
could have accomplished so much good in your life.

It's a lovely present tense, isn't it?

Today's passage contains a promise Christ made to his disciples before he returned to his Father. Knowing our tendency
to forget, he promises a helper, the Holy Spirit. Different Bible
translations use *Helper*, *Comforter*, and *Advocate* to describe the
Holy Spirit. Each descriptor is rich in meaning, and we need the
Spirit to play all three roles in our lives.

As *Helper*, the Holy Spirit helps us to remember what Christ
has said to us. We need help because we are prone to forget all the
glorious truths about our present tense. Notice in the passage that
Christ does not condemn the disciples for forgetting. He doesn't
accuse them of absentmindedness. He doesn't chide them for
inevitably losing sight of the wonders they've witnessed in him.
He knows they will be forgetful, so he doesn't even mention their
forgetfulness. He just provides the solution.

But why will they forget what he said? Why will *we* forget

what he said? It's not just because we have limited mental capacity (though that is true!). This is the more frightening reason we forget: there are so many voices, and so many noises and distractions, that vie for our attention and allegiances. And these voices aren't benign, especially when you have a painful past. The shame you feel and the false messages you've believed can creep back so subtly that you might not even notice at first. And behind all this, you have an Enemy who is a liar. Satan would have you believe lies about God and yourself and forget what Christ has said.

This is why it is critical that we have a Helper who shepherds us into remembering, and remembering, and remembering again. The Holy Spirit is a *Comforter*, and in bringing Christ's words to your remembrance, he comforts you with his truth. You are comforted when you remember he is your *Advocate*. He is for you. When Satan accuses you, the Spirit defends you.

You will forget your present-tense realities. The past will rear its ugly head again. But God gave you a Helper so that you will remember that you are his beloved child. He gave you a Comforter to ease today's burdens. He gave you an Advocate who guards and protects who you are in Christ.

Reflect: Because the lies and messages about our pasts can creep back subtly, we must name them and consider them in the light of God's Word. Though they may feel powerfully true, God is the only one who has a perfect perception of reality. As his children, we are to submit to his perception and say in faith, "I believe this is true even if it doesn't feel true."

Act: Reread the Scripture passages from Day 14 through Day 19. Choose one that most resonates with you, and work on memorizing it. Memorization is one way to partner with the Spirit in helping you remember God's truth.

YOUR SECURE FUTURE

DAY 21

God Gives Reasons
to Not Lose Heart

*He who raised the Lord Jesus will raise us also with Jesus and bring us
with you into his presence. For it is all for your sake, so that as grace
extends to more and more people it may increase thanksgiving, to the
glory of God. So we do not lose heart. Though our outer self is wasting
away, our inner self is being renewed day by day. (2 Cor. 4:14–16)*

TODAY WE WILL start to look at the most significant time in
your life. It's the time that will extend into eternity—the future.
Just as God speaks about your past and present, he also has much
to say about your future. More than that, he *promises* much for
your future. Yesterday we thought about how the Holy Spirit helps
us remember all Christ has said and done. In this next section, we
will be intentional both to call to mind and to remember what
Scripture says about your future. We will practice remembering
what *will be* true of you in the future because you *are* in Christ in
the present. As we remember, I will continually point you to the
practice of *finding comfort* and *delighting* in what God promises to
do for you in the future. We will also consider some concerns you
may have about your future because of your painful past.

Today's passage starts us off with an event that is at the heart
of the Christian faith: Jesus's resurrection from the dead. If he was
not raised, then our faith is in vain (see 1 Cor. 15:14). But God
did raise him, and that means something for us. Because we are in
Christ, God will raise us too, and he will usher us into the presence of Christ. Because you are in Christ, your fate is tied to his.
He was already raised, so you can be certain—confident, assured,
convinced—that you too will be raised. And not only raised, but
alive with Christ himself.

What will that be like? God is love, so you will be raised to live in the presence of love. God is the Creator, so you will live among the glories and wonders of his creative power. God is your Father, so you will live with the One who knows you most and adores you to your depths, and you'll live with your brothers and sisters in his family. God is the Redeemer of the world, so you will live as a fully healed, fully whole person. We could go on. I trust you see the point. These are rich realities to look forward to. They are reasons to not lose heart today or tomorrow.

The passage then circles around to a present-day promise: your inner self is being renewed day by day. This goes hand in hand with the fact that "the old has passed away" (2 Cor. 5:17). God's activity in your life is not only to carve away what needs to go. He is also creating newness within you that will bloom and flourish for all eternity.

We're just getting started. Tomorrow we will move forward with the next two verses in this passage.

Reflect: When you think about being in God's presence, what comes to mind?

Act: Using the pattern above, *God is _____, so you will be _____,* come up with your own similar statements, considering who he is and what it will be like to be in his presence. For example, *God is the Good Shepherd, so I will be . . .* or *God is the Healer, so I will be . . .* Ask God to help you remember these for times when you are losing heart.

Act: Listen to the hymn "Through the Love of God Our Savior" by Mary Bowley Peters. Notice how she points us to find comfort during tribulations by calling to mind future realities: "all will be well." Learning to find comfort and delight in the future God has prepared for his people will serve you well when you are hurting.

DAY 22

The Glories to Come

*For this light momentary affliction is preparing for us an eternal
weight of glory beyond all comparison, as we look not to the
things that are seen but to the things that are unseen.
For the things that are seen are transient, but the things
that are unseen are eternal. (2 Cor. 4:17–18)*

TODAY'S PASSAGE PRESENTS a challenge by calling our
afflictions "light and momentary." When you're in the middle of
affliction, or you've had more than your fair share of it in your
past, "light" and "momentary" definitely do *not* capture what that
feels like. Has the Bible misunderstood our experience of suffering? Does God not know what it is like for us to live with the
repercussions and wounds of a painful past? Before we dismiss
this passage as out of touch and move on, let's see if there is more
for us to understand.

How can our past and present afflictions be considered light
and momentary? Our afflictions *do* have weight. They are heavy.
But when weighed against our future glory, our afflictions can
rightly be considered light in comparison. "Momentary" also car-
ries the notion that afflictions do occur but do so *in passing*, which
again reinforces the Bible's comforting refrain that the hard things
we face are passing away. They are real, yes. They are painful to
endure, absolutely. But more can be said, and more must be said.
Remember, our laments must go somewhere good because God
has chosen to move into our lives. There is more that is true. It's
just harder for what is true to resonate with us because it is not
yet in our experience. We must accept truth *by faith*—believing
in what we cannot yet see and what we have not yet experienced
as true. A lament ends with trust and thanksgiving as we inwardly

confirm God's promises. We do this by our personal response of *yes* and *amen* to what God has done for us.

The apostle Paul penned today's verses. As someone who bravely faced many miseries in his life, he encourages us to look not at what we can see but at what is unseen. Why? Because what we can see is temporary, but what we can't see is eternal. Oh, what wonderful news! Much that we see is ugly, broken, wounded, bleeding, dying. It's hideously real, but it is all passing away. What we cannot yet see is the glory that is beautiful, whole, healed, bright, and bursting with life.

Lord, hurry and bring the day when our faith shall be sight!

Reflect: Speak this truth to yourself. Say it out loud. Repeat it: "The glory I will experience in my future will be so *overwhelmingly incredible* that I will not even dare compare it with the troubles I have gone through in my past and struggle with now." Now meditate on it. Start to enjoy it. Savor it. And be delighted by it.

Act: As we've reflected on what we cannot yet see, it's easy to understand the prayer of "I believe; help my unbelief!" (Mark 9:24). It's no small task to remain oriented to what God says is true and will be true when we have not yet seen or tasted it. Will you pray today about what makes it hard for you to trust that your afflictions are light and momentary? Will you confess how hard it is to have faith in what you can't see and ask God to help you to believe, and keep believing, until your faith becomes sight?

DAY 23

How to Think Biblically
about Yourself

For I am the least of the apostles, unworthy to be called an apostle,
because I persecuted the church of God. But by the grace of God I am
what I am, and his grace toward me was not in vain. (1 Cor. 15:9–10)

THE PAST TWO days, we've begun to consider some of the
future realities you can look forward to as God's child. At this
point, you might be thinking something like "OK, so I'm glad—
or at least trying to be glad—about the future I will have because
I am a Christian. But my past still exists, so how do I hold together
the realities of my past, present, and future?" This is a good question to consider because what happened in your past matters. Our
faith leads us to honestly and accurately assess what is true, so it
would be wrong to take what happened and gloss over it, mini-
mize it, or just forget it. The key to moving forward is putting your
past in its proper place. Let's look at how the apostle Paul did it.

In today's passage, Paul says plainly what he did: "I persecuted
the church." Elsewhere, he shares that he was a "blasphemer, per-
secutor, and insolent opponent" (1 Tim. 1:13). Because of this,
he knows he is the "least" of the apostles and "unworthy" to be an
apostle. But pay special attention to where he goes next. Notice
his "but." He doesn't end his story with what he did or who he
was in the past. Instead, he says, *"But by the grace of God I am what*
I am, and his grace toward me was not in vain."

Do you see how he holds it together? "Yes, that happened in
my past, *but* God gave me his grace, and now I am an apostle."
Paul fully owns this new reality about himself. He has confirmed
within himself that yes, this is what God did, and he shares the
truth of it with others. This confirmation for himself and before

others guarantees that God's grace to him wasn't in vain. Paul is committed to not letting that happen. Isn't that interesting?

It would be easy to think we are just failures or damaged goods because of what we did or what was done to us. But if we dwell there, then it is as if God's grace to us lacks power. God gave his Son to give us new life. And if we hold on to that truth, receive it, and believe it, then our lament goes where it is supposed to go: we are grateful for what the Lord has done in our lives.

Will you ask God to help you to consider his grace to you to be a real, significant part of who you are and how you are to understand your story? Grace is his gift to you, and he longs for you to receive it.

Reflect: Our Day 19 passage was 1 Corinthians 1:26–31. Go back and reread it, paying attention to its own "but God" statement.

Act: Write out a short story of your past in the way Paul did. Start with "I was," "I did," or "I had this happen . . ." After that, transition to "but God," and make the critical shift to what he has done for you.

Act: Read Psalm 130. The psalmist is crying to God from "depths of woe." Notice how he moves through his lament and connects to the larger story of God's activity through his own "But with [God]" acknowledgment (v. 4). I want you to become an expert at moving in this same way.

DAY 24

What If the Past Repeats Itself?

The steadfast love of the LORD never ceases;
his mercies never come to an end; they are new every
morning; great is your faithfulness. (Lam. 3:22–23)

YESTERDAY WE CONTEMPLATED and savored the Bible's "but God" reassurances to us. Today I will address a question—a fear—that may be on your mind. It's the question "What if I repeat my past?" If your painful past was due to your own poor choices, you are aware of your ability to really mess things up. And if your painful past was a result of the sinful choices of others, you might wonder something like "What if someone hurts me again?"

In both cases, the past threatens to repeat itself. It's a dreadful thought, but God gives you resources to strengthen you for this possibility. Today's verse points us to them. Let's start at the end of the verse and work our way backward.

Great is God's faithfulness. He is faithful when we are not. He is faithful when other people are not. His faithfulness is great—greater than we can even imagine. We can trust in *his* character even when *we* have failed or when *others* have failed us.

God's mercies never come to an end; they are new every morning. If history repeats itself, you can count on the mercies of God meeting you right where you are each day. They will not run out. He will not run away. His mercies are so limitless that you can count on them—because you can count on God—to be there for you every day.

The steadfast love of the Lord never ceases. Notice the conditions here: there are none. God is love, so of course his love for you cannot stop. His love for you comes naturally to him.

If your past repeats itself in some way, big or small, this is where I want you to start: Look at what your God is like. He is faithful. He is merciful. He is love. Always and forever. And from there, *from the secure place of knowing that this is who he is and that he remains your Advocate,* receive his mercies and make good on them. If you have sinned in an all-too-familiar way, you can confess and repent. If you have been hurt in an all-too-familiar way, you can cry out for comfort from your Comforter. You can invite others into what is happening. Your God is with you, and you do not have to move forward on your own.

I pray you will recall today's meditation anytime you need it. But even now, you can be blessed because God has mercies for you today. He has mercies for you tomorrow. God's mercies will meet you every day in your future. Indeed, they extend into eternity itself. Great is his faithfulness to you!

Reflect: The hymn "Great Is Thy Faithfulness" is one saint's extended reflection on today's verse. Read the lyrics. What stands out? What can you thank God for? Now worship through this song. Find it online and sing with confidence because you can be confident that God is, and will be, faithful to you.

Act: Read Psalm 136. Repetition in Hebrew poetry emphasizes the importance of an idea. Take heart from the reassurances that the steadfast love of the Lord endures forever! The psalmist, like the author of today's passage, wants God's dear children to be comforted.

DAY 25

What Is—and Will Always Be—True about You?

Blessed be the God and Father of our Lord Jesus Christ, who has blessed us in Christ with every spiritual blessing in the heavenly places. (Eph. 1:3)

WE WHO HAVE painful pasts tend to think of ourselves exclusively in terms of the past: "This is what I did, so this is who I am," or, if you were victimized, "This is what was done to me, so this must be what I deserve."

But as we've discussed, it's important *not* to let our own view of ourselves go unchecked. We should ask, "What does God say is true about me?" The letter to the Ephesians gives us many ways to answer that question as Paul begins with an extended prayer of thanks for what Christ has done for us. Let's walk through his prayer with an eye on seeing what is true about you because of what Christ has done for you. The answers will tell you who you are today and who you will always be.

God blessed you in Christ with every spiritual blessing (v. 3). The verses that follow describe the spiritual blessings that have come from "the heavenly places" into your life. For now, notice *every.* God blessed you with *every* spiritual blessing.

God chose you (v. 4). He picked you, even when you thought your past could disqualify you. Over your lifetime and for all of eternity, God will choose to draw near to you again and again—and he will never question his choice.

You are holy (v. 4). Christ's holiness becomes yours because you are in him. To be holy is to be set apart for God's purposes. You will always be holy.

You are blameless (v. 4). The Son was perfect on your behalf. You might feel guilty, but you are actually guiltless. God holds nothing against you. You will always be blameless.

God adopted you (v. 5). You thought you were an outcast, but God brought you into his family. You are a treasured, valued child. You will always be in God's family.

You have redemption through Christ's blood (v. 7). Christ's death paid the ransom to God and bought you out of your slavery to sin. You will always live a redeemed life.

God forgave your trespasses (v. 7). Christ paid the penalty for every single one of your sins. Christ's record is yours—so your record is clean. You will always be forgiven.

God lavished his grace on you (v. 8). The word *lavished* exudes a sense of bounty. God's grace to you is copious. God's grace will always cover your life—today, tomorrow, and forever.

What's so lovely about this list is that God made all this true about you in *his wisdom* and *insight* (v. 8). As he took holy counsel within himself, he saw it was all-wise and all-insightful for these spiritual blessings to come to pass in your life. This is why we bless and praise him (v. 3). Making these truths true about you is all part of his plan (v. 10).

Where is this plan going? He reveals the future: he will unite all of us—all things in heaven and on earth—under Christ (v. 10).

Reflect: God made known the "mystery of his will" (v. 9). He *really* wants you to know the spiritual blessings he's graced you with and to receive, believe, trust, and delight in them. How can these blessings become the controlling realities in your life? What difference might it make for how you live your life today and tomorrow?

Act: Write out today's spiritual realities in the first person—for example, "God chose *me*. *I* am holy," and so on. How does it feel to see these realities about yourself in black and white in front of you?

DAY 26

God's View of You Will
Always Be True

In him we have obtained an inheritance, having been predestined according to the purpose of him who works all things according to the counsel of his will, so that we who were the first to hope in Christ might be to the praise of his glory. In him you also, when you heard the word of truth, the gospel of your salvation, and believed in him, were sealed with the promised Holy Spirit, who is the guarantee of our inheritance until we acquire possession of it, to the praise of his glory. (Eph. 1:11–14)

TODAY WE WILL finish Paul's opening prayer in his letter to the Ephesians. What does God say is true about you? Paul offers three additional ways our God is shaping and preparing you for a glorious future. Let's continue to go verse by verse.

You have obtained an inheritance (v. 11). Christ, the perfect Son, is the rightful heir of his Father's bounty (see Heb. 1:2). Christ has chosen to share his inheritance. He shares it with you and me. The King and Lord over all creation wants to share the fruit of his kingship and lordship with his family. *We* will one day reign with him in unity, love, justice, and peace.

God predestined you to be to the praise of his glory (vv. 11–12). In your future, you will be perfectly whole and complete—a radiant, unique reflection of the image of God. When your Father sees you, when your family sees you, we will praise the Lord for his work! Who you are will cause others to say, "Glory to God!" This is God's plan for you; in fact, he predestined this coming reality. Predestination is mysterious, but take comfort that what you've done or experienced in the past could not, and did not, thwart this future for you.

You are sealed with the Holy Spirit (v. 13). Yesterday we saw that God's plan is to unite all things under Christ. So it makes sense that as a foretaste of that plan, Christ would send the Spirit to seal you. This seal, this yoking that he's made between you and him, is a guarantee that all these blessings will be fully realized in your future. You have a guarantee. Sit with that a moment. God has guaranteed that you will "acquire possession" of your inheritance. Not only has he accomplished salvation for you, he has also shared his inheritance with you, *and* he wants you to be confident that it will all come to pass as he promised.

Receive these gifts, which Christ has prepared and shared with you. The brightness of your eternal future is God's comfort for you today and every day.

Reflect: Even though we won't be able to imagine all that our eternal future will be like, we can imagine some of it. Imagine it now. Imagine being united to your Father and spiritual family. What will it be like? What will it feel like? What will it sound like?

Act: Write out today's three spiritual realities in the first person—for example, "*I* have obtained an inheritance . . ." Thank God for making these realities true about you.

Act: On Day 15, you wrote the story you tell yourself about yourself. Compare that story to the list we've constructed over the past two days. What are the differences? Ask God to help you to trust that the spiritual realities tell the true story about who you are.

DAY 27

Your God Will Be
Your Forever Home

*"In my Father's house are many rooms. If it were not so, would I have told
you that I go to prepare a place for you? And if I go and prepare a place
for you, I will come again and will take you to myself, that where I am you
may be also. And you know the way to where I am going." (John 14:2–4)*

WE ARE CONTINUING to think about your eternal future. On
your own, you would stay oriented to your past, and its presence
in your life would continue to surround you with the stench of
death. But you are not on your own. You have life today. Because
of Christ, you have a bright today and even brighter tomorrows
to eagerly anticipate. Today we'll consider yet another brightness
in your future.

Today's verses are from the conversation in which Jesus pre-
pares his disciples for his departure and offers them comfort.
One way Jesus comforts his disciples—and us—is by sending his
Helper (see John 14:26). In today's passage, Christ offers another
comfort. This comfort gives them—and us—hope for the future.

Jesus explains that it is good that he return to the Father because he will prepare a place for the disciples in one of the many
rooms in his Father's house. Jesus uses the same word for *house*
that he used in John 8:35 when he said, "The slave does not remain in the house forever; the son remains forever." Taking these
two verses together, we can conclude that this house is special
because it is where Jesus will be permanently. And if Jesus is there,
then all those whom God has brought into the family will be
there as well. Forever.[1] The emphasis is on *permanence*. This place
with God that Jesus is preparing for you will be your permanent
home—your forever home.

What is this home like? Many Christians over the centuries have debated whether Jesus was talking about literal rooms in actual houses. But remember, God's plan is to bring all things to unity under Christ (see Eph. 1:10). Therefore, there is biblical precedent to see these dwelling places as a metaphor for the permanent union we will have with our Father through our union with Jesus. Just as Jesus leaves to go unite with his Father, we, too, will be united with him one day.[2]

And when you are united to your Father, *he* will be your home. Your eternal home is with God your Father. Your eternal home is in Christ his Son. This is better than any mansion with dozens of rooms. He is better than any mansion. And you have a place with him. Wherever he is, there you will be, too. Permanently united. Permanently home.

Reflect: A stanza in the hymn "O Come, O Come, Emmanuel" sings,

> O come, thou Key of David, come
> And open wide our heav'nly home;
> Make safe the way that leads on high,
> And close the path to misery.[3]

Reflect on all Jesus is to us: he is our home, and he is the key to our home. He is the way to our home (see John 14:6). When you arrive, he will permanently close the path to misery. You will be forever safe with him.

Act: Today's passage offers us another way to think about "O Come, O Come, Emmanuel." While the original song of course had Jesus's first coming in mind, we now await Jesus's second coming. Find this hymn online and worship by singing it as a forward-looking prayer for Jesus to come again and unite you permanently to your Father (see v. 3).

DAY 28

One Day You Will Be
Fully Transformed

See what kind of love the Father has given to us, that we should be called children of God; and so we are. The reason why the world does not know us is that it did not know him. Beloved, we are God's children now, and what we will be has not yet appeared; but we know that when he appears we shall be like him, because we shall see him as he is. And everyone who thus hopes in him purifies himself as he is pure. (1 John 3:1–3)

TODAY'S PASSAGE REINFORCES truths we've pondered earlier, and it adds to our growing understanding of what our future will be like.

This will be familiar by now: God declares you are his child. When the One with all authority says you are his child, then it is so. He made you his child as an act of love for you. And though we are already children, all that we will be is not yet so. We will undergo a future transformation: when we come face to face with our Savior, we will be like him.

You will be like Christ. God could bestow no greater honor on you than to make you like his beloved Son. He who is most honorable honors you. *Oh, humble God, who are we that you would make us like your Son?!* Yet isn't it just like our God to do such a thing? After all, Jesus did not count equality with God something to grasp but made himself nothing so that you could turn away from your past and turn toward him (see Phil. 2:6–7), so that you could one day both see him and become like him.

Let's say it again: you will be like him. Today, we have the Holy Spirit, who helps us obey Christ and produce the fruit of the Spirit. But in the future, when we become fully like Christ, the fruit of the Spirit will be second nature to us. We won't be tempted to live in any way that does not conform to the will of our good, kind Father.

And there's more. When you put your hope in him, it purifies you because he is pure. What can we make of this? The answer may partially lie in how we respond to what he has done for us. When we take in and consider all God has gifted to us in Christ, our natural response is to worship him. And as we worship him, as we appreciate who he truly is, then a natural desire arises to be like him. His purity motivates us to image him. As we imitate him, it purifies us. And, indeed, we are told to imitate him (see Eph. 5:1). There is no one else we'd rather be like.

This is the regard God shows you: he will make your transformation into the image of his Son complete. Today's passage points to that day in your future. You will come face to face with him who is pure, and you will be purified in that instant. Your faith will become sight. Forevermore, you will be like Christ.

Reflect: Though we don't know what it will be like to be completely changed and like Christ, it's good to use our God-given imaginations and picture what it will be like. What characteristics of Christ do you look forward to expressing perfectly?

Act: Though you won't do so completely or perfectly, you are called to imitate Christ, and even today, united to the Holy Spirit, you *can* imitate Christ. This is an honor in your life for today and every day in your future. How can you be like Christ today in whatever circumstances are happening in your life?

DAY 29

Jesus Will Wipe Away Your Tears

"He will wipe away every tear from their eyes, and death shall be no more, neither shall there be mourning, nor crying, nor pain anymore, for the former things have passed away." (Rev. 21:4)

CRYING. WEEPING. ACHING. Groaning. Grieving. Hurting. Suffering.

This outpouring of agonizing emotions goes hand in hand with your painful past. You have done important work throughout this devotional, but that doesn't mean these difficult emotions and experiences will completely go away. There may be seasons in your life in which you will need to process again what happened and how it has impacted you. There may be consequences or wounds from your past that you don't fully shed in this life. That is why I subtitled this book *Healing and Moving Forward*. God doesn't usually heal us all at once, but he does initiate the process of healing, and he will continue to walk with you through it. Though it may be ongoing, God is in this process with you, so you can trust that you are moving *forward*. God is taking you somewhere good. You are never stagnant because you have a Shepherd who joins you on the journey and guides you. Today's passage gives us another glimpse of where he is bringing you.

Usually we wipe away our own tears. Rarely is someone physically close enough to us or so relationally intimate with us that they'd reach over and wipe away our tears. But this God knows you. And knowing you, he loves you. Don't miss his tenderness here. He will come close to you and wipe away your tears. *All* your tears. All the tears from a past with hurt, disappointment, regret, shame, and fear. All the tears that come with death, mourning, suffering, and pain. How is this possible? How can he wipe them away permanently? Because the "former things have passed away." You will have begun a new era of living, one in which death, mourning, suffering, and pain have no place and so will be no more. One in which you will be healed once and for all. You won't need to sort out your past anymore. You will move forward into your eternity whole and joyous, complete and content.

Gratitude will be our predominant experience at that point because none of this future could have been possible without the intervening, sacrificial, saving, keeping work of Jesus Christ. He made it possible for this moment to arrive. He has guaranteed that your past is fully passed away. He used his power on your behalf to do what you could not do.

And so it's his hand that reaches out to you and lovingly wipes away that last tear.

Reflect: Sometimes I find these future spiritual realities overwhelming. It's as if they are too good to be true. No more pain and suffering? The God who died for me gently wiping away my final tears? Somehow God's promises go straight to our deepest desires and our wildest dreams. But upon further reflection, this makes sense because God made us. And he made us for him. So of course our deepest desires will be fulfilled in our relationship with him. He will fulfill our deepest desires as he ushers us into an eternity in which we will experience life as he intends it to be.

Act: Today's verse is from Revelation 21. Read the whole chapter to get a fuller picture of what God showed John of the new heaven. After you read, close your eyes and imagine the details that John describes. Finally, pray about what comes to your mind and heart as you consider these future glories.

DAY 30

How Will God Use Your Story?

*Blessed be the God and Father of our Lord Jesus Christ, the Father
of mercies and God of all comfort, who comforts us in all our
affliction, so that we may be able to comfort those who are in any
affliction, with the comfort with which we ourselves are comforted by
God. For as we share abundantly in Christ's sufferings, so through
Christ we share abundantly in comfort too. (2 Cor. 1:3–5)*

THE ETERNAL GOD took on our likeness and came to earth
in vulnerability as a newborn baby. Jesus came on a mission to
reconcile all things to himself (see 2 Cor. 5:19). For this reason,
we are comforted as we remember that we're not just living in
our own story and alongside the stories of other hurting people.
Another person's story burst into this world when Immanuel
came to be with us. His story—what he did and what it means
for you—gives you every good reason to be comforted. And God
wants you to be comforted. He is your Father, your Friend, your
Advocate, and he is not indifferent to what troubles you, including your painful past. Treasure this.

As you treasure Christ and his love, as you are comforted because you trust that he loves you, you can comfort others with
the same truths that bring you relief. This is one way God will
use your story. You have a painful past, but that is not the only
true thing about you. Others in your life may have painful pasts,
but that is not the only true thing about them. This is also true:
we live in a time when God is calling out to the world that he
has mercies and comfort for all who hear his voice and respond.
This is the comfort of the gospel message. It is good news for the
whole world. And it is good news that is personal.

Though the message goes far and wide, it touches down in the lives of individual people and meets us in the details. God has met you in the details of your life. He has offered you personal comfort for the pain your past brings. And at some point you will have the opportunity to give that comfort to others. This is a sweet and honored privilege: the Lord of comfort uses his people whom he has comforted to bring his comfort to others. To bless one another with Christ's comfort is characteristic of our family. It's a normal activity for us. Though tears still come now, we wipe them away with hope because of the promise that one day Christ will wipe them all away forever. When you see the tears of others, the pain of others, you can wipe them away—literally or metaphorically—by recalling and pointing to the Christ who has brought you comfort and extends his comfort to others through you.

You have a ministry of comfort.

Reflect: When you think about what happened in your past, how has God comforted you? Try to be as specific as possible. What in particular about who he is and how he has impacted your life brings you comfort?

Act: Take a few minutes to write down how God has ministered his comfort to you. Practice putting it into words so that you are prepared to put it to words for someone else one day.

DAY 31

Jesus Will Be Faithful
to the End

*Now may the God of peace himself sanctify you completely,
and may your whole spirit and soul and body be kept blameless
at the coming of our Lord Jesus Christ. He who calls you
is faithful; he will surely do it. (1 Thess. 5:23–24)*

OUR FINAL PASSAGE is from the apostle Paul as he ends his letter to the church in Thessalonica. In his last words, he both blesses and encourages his brothers and sisters.

Let me emphasize aspects of both his blessing and his encouragement to end our devotional.

First, Paul gives a blessing: *May God sanctify you completely. May God keep you blameless.* Paul knows that his readers are on the path to complete sanctification and blamelessness. It is the trajectory of those who are in Christ. What we will be is not yet fully realized; hence his use of the word *may*, as in, "May God do this work that is not yet complete."

Second, Paul offers us reassurance. You might be thinking, "But doesn't saying '*may* God' do these things imply that he *might not*?" The answer is no. God will assuredly sanctify you and keep you blameless. How can we know this for sure? Because of who God is. *He who calls you is faithful.* God faithfully keeps his people. God will faithfully keep you, and he will keep you for today, for all of your future days, and for all of your eternity. *He will surely do it.*

Paul is as confident here as he can be: he says *surely.* There is no room for doubting that you are safe, and will be safe, when a faithful Father keeps watch over you.

Let's consider his keeping work in terms of where we have been together the past thirty-one days.

You have a *painful past*—and the Lord kept your life so that your past did not ruin you or define what your tomorrows could be.

You have a *transformed present*—because the Lord is keeping you today and extends new mercies to you every morning. Jesus gave you his Spirit, who is with you today, giving you power to live in your new story with faith and trust.

You have a *secure future*—because the Lord will keep his promises to you.

He kept you, he keeps you, and he will keep you. He will keep your coming in and your going out from this moment on and forevermore.

Surely, he will do it.

Reflect: When we trust who God is, it is clear why we would want him to "keep" us. As you think about what happened in your past, how is it helpful to consider yourself someone who has been, who is, and who will be *kept* by God?

Act: Read Psalm 121 in an ESV Bible. Notice the six uses of "keep." This repetition means the psalmist really wanted to emphasize this aspect of how God relates to us. God wants you to know that he keeps you so that you trust that you are safe and secure.

Conclusion

THANK YOU, DEAR reader, for the time you invested in this devotional. You have done important work, and I trust that God has met you in these devotional times. I believe he ministered to you because his heart is wedded to yours. You are his beloved child, and when his children show up needy and searching, he is there.

As you go from here, let me offer you a few thoughts.

First, *there is no silver bullet to healing.* This devotional may have been the first time you reckoned with your past. Or perhaps you have already wrestled and fought for freedom, and this devotional was another way you worked toward healing.

If you are just getting started, perhaps this devotional can be a jumping-off point to continue to press into healing. The conversation between you and God about your past has begun, and you now know that he invites you to speak. So keep speaking to him. Perhaps you will keep the conversation going, too, with trusted friends, your small group, or a counselor. You may also consider the suggested resources I have listed for you.

Or perhaps you have reached the end of this book feeling peaceful about your past. I am deeply thankful if that is the case. But I also want you to know that there may be a time in the future when the implications of what happened in the past come up again. This can happen as a result of significant life transitions, new situations that bring up old memories, or ongoing fallout from past events. Please be open to revisiting what happened in your past and how it impacted you. There is no shame in finding yourself in a new season in which you need to process again what happened in the past. Your compassionate Companion will walk you where you need to go.

All of us need to repeat, rehearse, and remember the spiritual realities and promises that God has revealed to us in his Word. Let's be in the habit of casting our gaze, our thoughts, and our ears toward our God. Let's listen again and again to what he has to say. His words are life. His words are true. And we need his life-giving words to both comfort us through the trials and carry us through the temptations that we face as we journey to our permanent home.

Second, let me make explicit an aspect of this book that was implicit throughout: *a core, fundamental way to heal is to worship your God.* We worship because God is worthy, yes and amen. But we must also worship because our lives depend on it. We must worship because if our lives center around ourselves, what we've done, and what happened in our pasts, then we are on the path toward death. But when we worship the one true God, our lives revolve around him and what he has done, and then we are on the path toward life, and life everlasting. This is why I have emphasized the new story you are now living in. Get situated, get comfortable, get settled in Christ's story because it's the new story that defines your life. This is why the Bible speaks of being born again. We must die to ourselves and our old ways of living so that we can live anew in Jesus's story. To some, dying to ourselves sounds like a burden. For those of us with a painful past, we must take it for what it is—good news. We know firsthand how much hurt, misery, and brokenness exists and can be experienced in this life. We've lived through it. But in and through Christ, God gave us his remedy.

And on the cross, Jesus said, "It is finished."

His life was blotted out—so that your true life could appear.

His body was desecrated—so that you could be saved and raised.

His connection with his Father was broken—so that you could be united to your Father.

And so he brought you into his family, he shared who he is,

and he gives you what he has. Now his story is your inheritance. It's your guarantee. It's your heritage. The deepest and truest *you* is who you are in him. It is why you bear his name—you are a *Christ*ian. Your life has come not because you found yourself but because Another found you and brought you into himself.

Finally, my parting prayer for you is that *you grow in the knowledge of how much your God loves you*. A painful past threatens to obscure his love. The pain makes it harder to see, to grasp, and to receive his love. But God so deeply loves you. He is for you. The Maker of heaven and earth, of all that is seen and unseen, has given you his blessing. By his birth, death, and resurrection, Christ proclaims to you:

> I have blessed you, and I have kept you.
> I shine my face upon you.
> I am gracious to you—and I will be gracious to you.
> I lifted you into my very presence, and I will always, *always*,
>> give you my peace.[1]

Acknowledgments

I AM THANKFUL to Deepak Reju, who invited me to join this project. It was an honor to contribute to the larger series of books that aim to bring a balm to many of the issues Christians face. Thank you to Amanda Martin at P&R for her earnest and thorough editorial feedback.

I am thankful for the support of my colleagues at CCEF, who have prayed for and encouraged me. Thank you to my fellow counselors at CCEF. In our weekly meetings, you never fail to show me what it looks like to compassionately and graciously come alongside people who are hurting. Thank you to Jacklyn Tubel, whose faithful prayers covered this book over the many months during which I was working on it. Thank you to Ed Welch, who gave input at both the beginning and ending stages of the writing process. Thank you to Kim Monroe, who provided edits, love, and encouragement. Thank you to Esther Liu and Heather Quinlisk, who provided helpful comments that led to many improvements. Thank you to Jayne Clark, who has been a cheerleader of my counseling career ever since she met me when I was a graduate student. And thank you to the many counselees whom I have walked with over my years at CCEF. You have shown me what courage and faith look like in the midst of pain and heartache.

I would also like to express my gratitude for David Powlison, who passed away while I was writing this book. I had the privilege of working with David for almost ten years. During that time, David, Kim Monroe, and I worked together on about 150 articles for the *Journal of Biblical Counseling*. Not only did David teach me the art of editing, he also gave me numerous opportunities to develop as a writer. I learned much from him—and not just about writing. He showed me what it means to live like a Christian. He demonstrated how to bring the truth of God's Word into people's lives in a way that is lively and connects. Even while sick, David gladly read and provided feedback on my outline for this book. It is grief upon grief that he is not here now to celebrate its publication with me.

My final thanks go to my family:

To my parents and sister for your love that has covered every day of my life.

To my husband, Chad, for your unwavering support throughout this writing process. You've encouraged me for years to write and the book is here now because of your partnership, friendship, and love. I could not have done it without you. I cherish the life we built together.

And to my children. You are God's precious gifts to your father and me, and we treasure both of you. If you ever read this book, I hope you will be gripped by how much Jesus loves you and spurred on in your love for him. It is Jesus's love that was the vision and basis for every word I wrote.

Notes

Day 3: God Spends Time with Broken People

1. For an engaging explanation of the idea of God's holiness overcoming our unholiness, see "Holiness," BibleProject, video, 6:34, March 17, 2015, https://www.youtube.com/watch?v=l9vn 5UvsHvM.

Day 6: A Lament to the Lord

1. Christina Fox, "The Way of Lament," Ligonier Ministries, May 6, 2016, https://www.ligonier.org/blog/way-lament/.
2. Fox, "The Way of Lament."

Day 16: You Are in Christ

1. Adolphe Adam, "O Holy Night," 1847.

Day 18: You Are in God's Family

1. J. I. Packer, *Knowing God* (Downers Grove, IL: InterVarsity, 1973), 201.
2. Horatio Spafford, "It Is Well with My Soul," 1873.

Day 27: Your God Will Be Your Forever Home

1. Raymond E. Brown, *The Gospel According to John (XIII–XXI)*, The Anchor Bible 29A (Garden City, NY: Doubleday, 1970), 627.
2. Brown, 627.
3. "O Come, O Come, Emmanuel," trans. John Mason Neale, 1861.

Conclusion

1. This blessing is based on the priestly prayer of Numbers 6:24.

Suggested Resources
for the Journey

Huie, Eliza. "Should I See a Counselor?" *Journal of Biblical Counseling* 30, no. 2 (2016): 82–85. [This article walks you through six considerations to help you answer the question, Should I see a counselor? There are seasons in life when it may be very helpful to seek formal counseling help. As someone who has personally benefitted from counseling, I encourage others to be open to exploring the option.]

Ortlund, Dane. *Gentle and Lowly: The Heart of Christ for Sinners and Sufferers*. Wheaton, IL: Crossway, 2020. [This book is a lovely, extended meditation on who Christ actually is.]

Powlison, David. *God's Grace in Your Suffering*. Wheaton, IL: Crossway, 2018. [This book explores how God meets us and transforms us even in the midst of difficult suffering.]

———. "'I'll Never Get Over It'—Help for the Aggrieved." *Journal of Biblical Counseling* 28, no. 1 (2014): 8–27. [This is an article for those who have suffered grievous wrongs. Will you ever get over it? Powlison locates a redemptive way forward and includes questions at the end to personally consider.]

Welch, Edward T. *Shame Interrupted: How God Lifts the Pain of Worthlessness and Rejection*. Greensboro, NC: New Growth Press, 2012. [How does God lift the pain of shame? In this thoroughly biblical book, Welch points to the ways in which Jesus definitively and permanently covered our shame by taking shame upon himself.]

Restoring Christ to Counseling and Counseling to the Church

COUNSELING
ccef.org/counseling

WRITING
ccef.org/resources

TEACHING
ccef.org/courses

EVENTS
ccef.org/events

"CCEF is all about giving hope and help with a 'heart.' If you want to learn how to effectively use God's Word in counseling, this is your resource!"

Joni Eareckson Tada, Founder and CEO, Joni and Friends International Disability Center

"The vision of the centrality of God, the sufficiency of Scripture, and the necessity of sweet spiritual communion with the crucified and living Christ—these impulses that lie behind the CCEF ministries make it easy to commend them to everyone who loves the Church."

John Piper, Founder, desiringGod.org; Chancellor, Bethlehem College & Seminary

---

Christian Counseling & Educational Foundation
ccef.org

More from P&R Publishing for Your Encouragement

Why do Christians—even mature Christians—still sin so often? Why doesn't God set us free? Speaking from her own struggles, Barbara Duguid turns to the writings of John Newton to teach us God's purpose for our failure and guilt—and to help us adjust our expectations of ourselves. Rediscover how God's extravagant grace makes the gospel once again feel like the good news it truly is!

"Take this book to heart. It will sustain you for the long haul, long after the hyped-up panaceas and utopias fail."
  —David Powlison

"Buy this book. Buy one for a friend and live in the freedom that only the good news of the gospel can bring."
  —Elyse Fitzpatrick

Was this book helpful to you?
Consider writing a review online.
The author appreciates your feedback!

Or write to P&R at editorial@prpbooks.com
with your comments. We'd love to hear from you.